Opening Fear
(Abro el Miedo)

poems by Teresa Orbegoso

translated by
Vania Milla

preface by
Margarita Saona

foreword by
Yaxkin Melchy

afterword by
Silvia Goldman

illustrations by
Louise Castillo

Dulzorada Press

OPENING FEAR

Originally published as *Abro el Miedo* in Peru (Hanan Harawi, 2019) and Argentina (Las Furias Editora, 2020)

© 2023, Dulzorada Press
Editor-in-chief: José Garay Boszeta | jose@dulzorada.com
Book design and layout: Miguel Garay Boszeta | miguel@dulzorada.com
Development manager: Melanie Cambiaso | mela@dulzorada.com
Dulzorada logo design: Bidkar Yapo | @nacionchicha.pe

Library of Congress Control Number: 2023940630

ISBN: 978-1-953377-25-8 (paperback)
ISBN: 978-1-953377-43-2 (hardcover)

Published by Dulzorada Press
http://Dulzorada.com

Printed in the USA

Opening Fear / Abro el Miedo

Opening Fear is a remarkable book: for its overwhelming power and for its language, beautiful in its raw truth, lucid, audacious, of great richness. It is a book about pain, but Teresa Orbegoso is a well-rounded poet, so she does not write a catharsis or an incantation but a book of poems. "Pain falls in love with words because it needs them," I once wrote. And that is how pain makes a nest in the poem, settles there to obtain certainty, the certainty of shelter and existence. "Whatever exists"; that is asked of her by her disease, with which she establishes an intimate, essential dialogue. Many Teresas inhabit this book, many of her universes: childhood; love for her country and the painful history it carries; rebellion against the injustices of the world; her defense of the most vulnerable. The book is imbued with urgency, with vertigo; we read it in an almost hypnotic state, unable to leave it and when we close it, our hands still trembling, we see that it embraces us, it binds us as sisters in its deep humanity, its wisdom and passion for life. *Opening Fear* is not just a book, it is a cameo to treasure.

— PAULINA VINDERMAN, POET AND TRANSLATOR, ARGENTINA

Opening Fear is not only contingent on a personal experience, but superimposes the physical body over the experiential body of a woman and the body of the continent that shelters her, all of them intensely political bodies, due to their intrinsic condition at the margins and in displacement. *Opening Fear* is a book that places us within pain, but also within the hope of healing. We think in one of the forms that Spinoza, read by Deleuze, shows as a way to reflect about the body: this is the threefold denunciation of conscience, values and sad affections. Body and soul cannot be dissociated. However, there is potency when the body becomes an object seen from a distance. One becomes aware of its existence and its pains. But even at that distance, one cannot know exactly what the potential is. Deleuze says: "What does Spinoza mean when he invites us to take the body as a model? It is a matter of showing that the body surpasses the knowledge that we have of it, and that thought likewise surpasses the consciousness that we have of it."

— CAMILA ALBERTAZZO, PROFESSOR AND PHILOSOPHER, CHILE

CONTENTS

What is the meaning of writing and poetry when one is sick?: on Teresa Orbegoso's *Opening Fear*
by Yaxkin Melchy Ramos-Yupari

I have been invited by Teresa to write a commentary on her powerful book of poems, *Opening Fear*. As I write this I am sick with coronavirus. The book is accompanying me during a hot summer in Japan and reading it places me in front of a naked reality, a reality with those moments of suffering, uncertainty and questioning that arise in our hearts when our "normal" life is disrupted by any disease. Even more so when this disease puts us on the edge of our own life as in the case of cancer. Teresa's book is a song from the heart and the body at the edge of one's own life, and it makes me wonder: What is the meaning of writing and poetry when one is sick?

I have once heard someone say that surviving cancer is learning to live with cancer. It seems that cancer has become one of the representative diseases of the 21st century and it is no exaggeration to say that we all know someone who has had some type of cancer. This reminds me of my friends in Mexico and Japan, close friends, female and male teachers, the uncertainty on their faces, the battles being waged between depression and hope. Once again the question appears before me, what is the meaning of writing and poetry when one is sick? But the truth is that Teresa Orbegoso's book directs us to a more basic question: What does cancer tell us about the world we live in? What does cancer tell us about our own lives?

As a starting point, I open the book to listen to what cancer has to say. Yes, cancer speaks, Teresa tells us, not only in the cells of the body but also as a worldwide disease with a psychic and spiritual existence. To listen to it we must open our hearts, open the fear that deafens us. That is the first step, the courageous step that poetry has to take in the face of illness. The disease has a voice, that is why the poet takes up the verse of the Chilean poet Gonzalo Millán that says: *"Talk to your cancer. Ask questions to that swarm of deranged cells"*, recorded in the book *Veneno de escorpión azul* (Blue Scorpion Venom), a poetic diary written during his illness, which in his case turned out to be terminal.

By listening and talking to the disease, *Opening Fear* shows us an outpouring of personal memories, family stories and landscapes from an affective geography of South America that goes from Tierra del Fuego to Alaska. Teresa does not abandon herself to just one of these outpourings but, echoing the voices of Inger Christensen's poems *Alphabet* and *It*, she allows them to run their course, to flow like a river that reveals something deeper, an incessant stream of "that which exists". She tells us to listen to "the particles that rule the world", listen to the "tangos and huaynos", listen to "the migration of pollen", listen to pain and hate because they all exist.

The dialogue with the disease also brings to the surface a geography of poetic speech. In *Opening Fear* the poet vindicates the poetic and sensitive existence of the South of the Americas. It is a speech that stands out for its rhythm and the use of threaded-verses that interweave with one another in a long poetic braiding:

The Americas exists
aymara exists; and the potato flower, the potato flower
and quechua exist; and Resígaro, Resígaro
alpacas exist; Resígaro, air;
and quinua fields exist; alpacas exist;
alpacas, abarema, aiphanes, arteries
capybaras exist; the mayans, the llicllas

10

the orejones exist; the capybaras, the capybaras
yana wayra, Mummy Juanita and the intis; the intis
exist.

Throughout several passages of *Opening Fear*, the dialogue with cancer reveals the existence of a continent made of ancient, indigenous, colonial, modern, globalized and popular fragments. The cancer incarnated in the poet's body dialogues with the world of the South of the Americas, both in the poems on each page and the poetic commentaries that appear as if they were footnotes.

The prophetic voice is also present. *Opening Fear* is a poetic revelation, a revelation that the poet receives from the world (our world) and from her own life. It is impossible not to read this book of poems without feeling the echo of the voice of the prophets and a clamor to God. Amid hospital wards and the noise of cities, cancer spreads over the Earth and reveals itself as an invasive force that seeks to supplant the word of God by saying "I was in the beginning as was the word." This tension between religious faith and the voice of disease is settled when the poet announces the assertion of healing: *"The cure exists, the cure exists/ the tiny embroidery on my grandmother's jute dress/ Everything as clean as it was in the beginning."* The poet renounces the forces of sinking and shipwreck: *"It is useless to plunge into ourselves as if into an abyss"*, in order to surrender her own word to a vital force impregnated with a spirit of immortality. She tells us:

it is useless to plunge into ourselves as if into an abyss

we have been abandoned in a strange movement
here the eternity of the hunger tree is naked,
it protects the bird,
says goodbye to war and disease
and the word that still remains in me
I detach it from my tongue
to give as a gift to the water spring

11

But I open a hole in my immortal cells. I draw at its beginning, I scribble at its end. I twist the paper on which I write their names, turn them into airplanes, into pigeons.

Finally, I want to emphasize that the last part of the poem is a wonderful poetic weaving and visual performance of the written word as a suture. The silence-chest, the white space, is like flesh upon which the poetic text is stitched. In the suture, some stitches are the things of the world and other stitches are words linked to affection, such as love, friendship, passion, beauty, evil and volition. The poem is the thread that binds them together upon the body-voice of the survivor. At the end of the poem we witness the miracle of the word that has returned to life and gushes forth powerfully like a spring. Is this water not the water of life that we all cry out for in a sick world?

Opening Fear is a powerful song written from the intimate surrender to the disease, which reveals to us that cancer is not something that exists only in the cells, but also in the culture, in the city, in history, in information and in the things of this world. Cancer exists, COVID-19 exists, AIDS exists, they speak through our own histories. The meaning of writing in times of sickness is to reveal to us the glory of life.

Tsukuba, summer of 2023.

A los hombres, mujeres, niños, niñas y animales
que viven con cáncer.

To the men, women, boys, girls and animals
living with cancer.

OPENING FEAR

Teresa Orbegoso

Habla con tu cáncer. Hazle preguntas a ese
enjambre de células descarriadas...

Veneno de escorpión azul
Gonzalo Millán

Talk to your cancer. Ask questions to that
swarm of deranged cells...

Blue Scorpion Venom
Gonzalo Millán

"...las glaciaciones existen, las glaciaciones existen,

el hielo del océano Ártico y el hielo del martín pescador;
las cigarras existen; chicoria, cromo

y el iris amarillo-cromo, el azul; el oxígeno
sobre todo; existen también los témpanos del océano Ártico,
el oso polar existe, marcado como una piel
con número de identidad existe, condenado a su vida;
y la zambullida mínima del martín pescador en los arroyos

de marzo azules de hielo existe, si existen los arroyos;
si el oxígeno en los arroyos existe, el oxígeno
sobre todo; existe sobre todo donde existe el sonido i
de las cigarras, sobre todo donde existe el cielo
de la chicoria como azul turquesa diluido

en agua, el sol amarillo-cromo, el oxígeno
sobre todo; claro que existirá, claro
que existiremos, el oxígeno que respiramos existe,
adonis, lantana existen, y el interior celestial
del lago; una ensenada encerrada
con unos pocos juncos existirá, un ibis existe,
y los movimientos de la mente insuflados en las nubes
existen como remolinos de oxígeno en lo más hondo de la Estigia

y dentro del paisaje de la sabiduría la luz glacial,
el hielo idéntico a la luz, y en lo más hondo
de la luz glacial la nada, viva, intensa,
como tu mirada a través de la lluvia; esta fina
lluvia persistente que estiliza la vida, donde como un gesto
las catorce retículas del cristal existen, los siete
sistemas cristalinos, tu mirada como en la mía,

20

"...ice ages exist, ice ages exist,

ice of polar seas, kingfishers' ice;
cicadas exist, chicory, chromium

and chrome yellow irises, or blue; oxygen
especially; ice floes of polar seas also exist,
and polar bears, stamped like furs with their
identification numbers, condemned to their lives;
the kingfisher's miniplunge into blue-frozen

March streams exists, if streams exist;
if oxygen in streams exists, especially
oxygen, especially where cicadas'
i-sounds exist, especially where
the chicory sky, like bluing dissolving in

water, exists, the chrome yellow sun, especially
oxygen, indeed it will exist, indeed
we will exist, the oxygen we inhale will exist,
lacewings, lantanas will exist, the lake's
innermost depths like a sky; a cove ringed
with rushes, an ibis will exist,
the motions of mind blown into the clouds
like eddies of oxygen deep in the Styx

and deep in the landscapes of wisdom, ice-light,
ice and identical light, and deep
in the ice-light nothing, lifelike, intense
as your gaze in the rain; this incessant,
life-stylising drizzle, in which like a gesture
fourteen crystal forms exist, seven
systems of crystals, your gaze as in mine,

21

e Ícaro, Ícaro desamparado existe;

Ícaro envuelto en las alas de cera derretidas
existe, Ícaro pálido como un cadáver
vestido de civil existe, Ícaro en lo más bajo donde
las palomas existen; los soñadores, las muñecas
existen; el cabello de los soñadores con los mechones
del cáncer arrancados, la piel de las muñecas sujeta
con alfileres, el hupe de los misterios; y las sonrisas
existen, los hijos de Ícaro blancos como corderos
a través de la luz gris, claro que existirán, claro
que existiremos, y el oxígeno sobre el crucifijo del oxígeno;
como escarcha existiremos, como viento existiremos
como el iris del arcoíris en las resplandecientes excrecencias
de la hierba del rocío, hierbas de la tundra; como pequeños

existiremos, tan pequeños como un poco de polen en la turba,
como un poco de virus en los huesos, tal vez como peste de agua,
tal vez como un poco de trébol, arveja, un poco de camomila
expulsada al paraíso de nuevo perdido; pero la oscuridad
es blanca, dicen los niños, la oscuridad del paraíso es blanca…"

Alfabeto
Inger Christensen

* Christensen, Inger. *Alfabeto* (trad. Francisco J. Uriz). México: Sexto Piso, 2014.

22

and Icarus, Icarus helpless;

Icarus wrapped in the melting wax
wings exists, Icarus pale as a corpse
in street clothes, Icarus deepest down where
doves exist, dreamers, and dolls;
the dreamers, their hair with detached
tufts of cancer, the skin of the dolls tacked together
with pins, the dryrot of riddles; and smiles,
Icarus-children white as lambs
in greylight, indeed they will exist, indeed
we will exist, with oxygen on its crucifix,
as rime we will exist, as wind,
as the iris of the rainbow in the iceplant's gleaming
growths, the dry tundra grasses, as small beings

we will exist, small as pollen bits in peat,
as virus bits in bones, as water-thyme perhaps,
perhaps as white clover, as vetch, wild chamomile,
banished to a re-lost paradise; but the darkness
is white, say the children, the paradise-darkness is white..."

Alphabet
Inger Christensen

* Christensen, Inger. *Alphabet* (trans. Sussana Nied). New York: New Directions Publishing, 2001.

23

"Eso. Eso fue. Así empezó. Eso es. Continúa. Se mueve. Más allá. Nace. Deviene eso y eso y eso. Sigue más allá de eso. Deviene otra cosa. Deviene más. Combina otra cosa con más y sigue deviniendo otra cosa y más. Sigue más allá de eso. Deviene otra cosa diferente a otra cosa y más. Deviene algo. Algo nuevo. Algo incesantemente más nuevo. En el próximo ahora deviene tan nuevo como puede serlo cualquier cosa. Se pavonea. Pasea. Toca, es tocado. Atrapa material suelto. Va haciéndose más y más grande. Aumenta su seguridad al existir como más que él mismo, gana peso, adquiere velocidad, adquiere algo más en su velocidad, adelanta al otro, hace sufrir al otro, que se recoge, se absorbe, se le carga rápidamente con lo que llegó primero, que empezó tan aleatoriamente. Eso fue. Tan diferente ahora que ha empezado. Tan transformado. Ya una diferencia entre eso y eso porque nada es lo que fue. Ya tiempo entre eso y eso, entre aquí y allí, entre antes y ahora. Ya la extensión del espacio desde eso a otra cosa, a más, a algo, algo nuevo, como ahora, en este ahora, fue, como en este ahora es y seguirá siendo. Se mueve. Llena. Ya es lo suficientemente él mismo por dentro como para diferenciar entre exterior e interior. Juega, prueba fortuna, se arremolina. En lo exterior. Y se densifica en el interior."

Eso
Inger Christensen

* Christensen, Inger. *Eso* (trad. Francisco J. Uriz). México: Sexto Piso, 2015.

"It. That's it. That started it. It is. Goes on. Moves. Beyond. Becomes. Becomes it and it and it. Goes further than that. Becomes something else. Becomes more. Combines something else with more to keep becoming something else and more. Goes further than that. Becomes something besides something else and more. Something. Something new. Newer still. In the next now, becomes as new as it now can be. Imposes itself. Flaunts itself. Touches, is touched. Catches free material. Grows bigger and bigger. Builds itself up by being more than itself, gains weight, gains speed, gains more in its rush, gains on something else, passes something else, which is taken up, taken in, fast laden with what came first, so randomly begun. That's it. So changed now that it's begun. So transformed. Already a difference between it and it, for nothing is what it was. Already time between it and it, here and there, then and now. Already the span of space between it and something else, it and more, it and something, something new, which now, in this now, already has been, in the next now is and goes on. Moves. Fills. Is already enough itself for inside to differ from outside. Plays, shifts, eddies. Outside. And condenses inside.

It
Inger Christensen

* Christensen, Inger. *It* (trans. Sussana Nied). New York: New Directions Publishing, 2006.

CIRUGÍA / SURGERY

Mi cáncer dice:

acuérdate de mí ahora que eres adulta y que han llegado los tiempos en que el agua bendita es sólo agua. Los tiempos en que el hábito del santo ha sido abandonado en la playa. Los tiempos en que tu páramo se ha partido en dos.

Escucha todo lo que suena en tu cáncer. ¿Alguien podrá oírlo contigo?

My cancer says:
Remember me now that you are an adult, and the time has come when holy water is just water. The times when the saint's robe has been abandoned on the beach. The times when your wasteland has been split in two.

Listen to everything that sounds in your cancer. Will anyone be able to hear it with you?

Abro el miedo. Mi madre viaja sola sobre un iceberg. Dentro de él estoy yo congelada mirándolo todo.

Algo. Algo es. Un pezón estrujado. Inger, algo avanza por mi pecho hasta casi llegar al hueso. Se aferra a algo y algo y algo. No puede detenerse, como los sonámbulos. Se aferra a lo que encuentra. Se aferra más.

Opening fear. My mother travels alone on an iceberg. Inside it I am frozen, looking at it all.

Something. It is something. A squeezed nipple. Inger, something is moving across my chest until almost reaching the bone. It clings onto something and something and something. It cannot stop, just like sleepwalkers. It clings to whatever it finds. It's clinging tighter.

Sí Inger, el agua bendita de Santa Rosa de Lima existe
La fría herida detenida existe
con los mechones del cáncer arrancados existe
Teresa Orbegoso existe

Las células buenas se encuentran con las células malas en la danza de las
células. Hay una guerra. Las células buenas pierden. Las células malas colocan
su bandera de vencedoras sobre mi pecho.

Yes Inger, the holy water of Saint Rose of Lima exists
The cold arrested wound exists
with torn out cancer strands exists
Teresa Orbegoso exists

The good cells meet the bad cells in the dance of cells. There is a war. The good cells lose. The bad cells are hoisting their victory flag upon my chest.

Mi cáncer dice:

cose tu historia a la mía y encontrarás a una madre y a una hija y dentro de ellas una palabra como una penitencia que las alumbra. Alguna de las dos reconocerá que un día dijo: no vayas al matrimonio como la vaca al matadero. Sin saber. Empapándote con la sangre del miedo. Que no te convenzan con eso de que tu madre es el mejor esposo. Cuántas veces las abuelas han destruido sus cabezas. La enfermedad se extiende sobre tu vestido como una mancha de aceite con la que deberás luchar. A la vencedora se le dará una revelación y se le dará también una pureza nueva y al interior de esa nueva pureza como una luz intermitente, un canto que nadie conoce sino sólo la que lo recibe.

Algo se repite en otros cuerpos. Se desarrolla. Dice aquí estoy. Se anuncia. Se impone. Me causa dolor. Adquiere confianza y se reproduce. Marcha.

My cancer says:

stitch your story to mine and you will find a mother and a daughter and inside them a word like penance that illuminates them. One of them will acknowledge that one day she said: Don't go into marriage like a cow to the slaughterhouse. Without knowing. Drenching yourself in the blood of fear. Don't let them convince you that your mother is the best husband. How many times have grandmothers destroyed their heads. The disease spreads through your dress like an oil stain you will have to fight with. The victor will be given a revelation and she will also be given a new purity, and within that new purity, like a flashing light, a song that no one knows but the one who receives it.

Something repeats itself in other bodies. It develops. It says here I am. It announces its presence. It imposes itself. It causes me pain. It gains confidence and reproduces. It marches.

Abro el miedo. Tener corazón para la paz. Tener corazón para la peste. Conocer los dientes blancos y brillantes de la felicidad. Aprender a bordar con oro la justicia. La enfermedad como un movimiento regular, como la marcha de un ejército de neblinas. Una única Teresa entre los juguetes viejos de la única niña de la única ciudad sobreviviente de la última guerra. Cada instante un rito: un ruido continuo, el voto de las naciones enloquecidas y la violencia, pequeña huérfana que corre, corre contenta para clavar su aguja sin aviso sobre los cuerpos de las mujeres con cáncer. En este mundo, una gasa ensangrentada sobre el viento tiene el mismo peso que la verdad y la misericordia. Las riendas de la tranquilidad tiene la mano del que ignora a qué viene a la vida. Y en su cara aparecida la cara vacía de la bondad y sus doce hijos, que tampoco tienen nada. La música de los cortadores y los fórceps, su murmullo, como el silbido de una enfermera olvidada en los pasillos de un hospital. La gran sala del trabajo con sus médicos sindicalistas de paja, sus pacientes disecados y sus objetos polvorientos: entre ellos la gratuidad como muñecote de papel maché inclinada junto a un ecógrafo roto como rezando en silencio. Los libros de la salud esparcidos, párrafo a párrafo, sobre las llaves del padecimiento.

Inger, algo sigue tomando mis órganos. Algo es. Con mayor tamaño. Con mayor fuerza. Tan absoluto.

Opening fear. Having a heart for peace. Having a heart for plague. Knowing the bright white teeth of happiness. Learning to embroider justice with a gold thread. Sickness as a regular movement, like the march of an army of haze. The only Teresa among the old toys of the only girl in the only city surviving the last war. Every instant, a rite: a continual noise, the vow of maddened nations and violence, a little orphan who runs, runs elated to stick her needle without warning into the bodies of women with cancer. In this world, a bloody gauze on the wind has the same weight as truth and mercy. The reins of tranquility have the hand of the one who ignores what life comes to. And on her face appearing the empty face of kindness and her twelve children, who have nothing either. The music of scalpels and forceps, their murmur, like the whistling of a nurse forgotten in the corridors of a hospital. The great hall of labor with its straw-like unionized doctors, its mummified patients and their dusty objects: among them, the free-of-charge service like a huge paper mache doll kneeling next to a broken ultrasound machine as if praying in silence. The health books scattered, paragraph by paragraph, over the keys of suffering.

Inger, something keeps taking over my organs. It is something. Larger in size. Greater in strenght. Something so absolute.

39

Teresa Orbegoso existe
La paciente con cáncer existe
El amigo que le da un beso intempestivo para que ella recuerde la vida
Desaparecemos de la faz de la tierra
una tarde   una mañana   una noche   una madrugada
cualquiera   ya sea
que un sonido te golpee o
el remolino de las cosas te sumerja una noche cualquiera

Algo silba otra lengua y da órdenes. Algo microscópico que baila dentro de mí.
Una música disonante que no me dice nada: un absurdo.

Teresa Orbegoso exists
The cancer patient exists
The friend who gives her an untimely kiss so that she remembers life
We disappear from the face of the earth
one afternoon   one morning   one evening   one dawn
any given   whether it be
may a sound hit you or
the whirlwind of things may submerge you on any given night

Something whistles another tongue and gives orders. Something microscopic that dances inside me. A dissonant music that tells me nothing: an absurdity.

Mi cáncer dice:

tienes cuarenta años. La edad para ver aunque tú no lo quieras. La vida nos toma y nos deja caer. Yo no era la muerte. Y entonces tú caías y te mirabas así: caída, sin poder hacer nada. Tú: la huérfana. Te dabas cuenta de que la felicidad no era una máquina, ni un peluche, ni un animal.

Algo busca nuevas palabras. Me lleva al recuerdo desordenado de mi infancia. Rueda y rueda como una piedra que hace volteretas con mis miedos.

My cancer says:

you are forty years old. The age to see even if you don't want to. Life takes us and lets us fall. I was not Death. And then you fell, and you looked at yourself like this: fallen, unable to do a thing. You: the orphan. You realized that happiness was not a machine, nor a stuffed or living animal

Something searches for new words. It takes me to the messy memory of my childhood. It rolls and rolls like a stone doing somersaults with my fears.

Abro el miedo. Una mañana moriré. Y ese día podré al fin escuchar la última ópera de mis células. Ese día el universo será de agua y el sol será una pelusa que veo levantarse cuando tiendo mi cama. Del cáncer vengo y al cáncer voy: ¿bienaventuranza o enfermedad? Un tronco se parte entre las dos. Miro los libros pasar. Son títulos y nombres de autores que desconozco. Caigo sobre las jaulas de las gallinetas de mis vecinos, sobre los brazos de mi abuela, sobre la pista de cemento y sus rayas blancas, caigo en todos lados. ¿Quiero seguir en este mundo? Ensalivada está mi boca. Un torito de Pucará me protege. Mi vida como la suciedad que no puedo limpiar.

Algo adquiere forma, vida propia. Más consistente que mi propia forma, que mi propia vida. Invade. Grito primitivo que le canta a mi pecho y lo deforma. Se alimenta de mí para que él pueda existir como un Dios al que odio.

Opening fear. One morning I will die. And on that day, I will finally be able to listen to the last opera of my cells. That day the universe will be made of water and the sun will be a fuzz that I see rising when I make my bed. From cancer I come and to cancer I go: a blessing or a disease? A log splits between the two. I watch the books go by. They are titles and names of authors I don't know. I fall on top of the cages, on my neighbors' coops, on my grandmother's arms, over the cement track and its white stripes, I fall everywhere. Do I want to continue being in this world? My mouth is salivating. A little Pucara bull protects me. My life as the dirt I cannot clean.

Something takes shape, a life of its own. More consistent than my own form, than my own life. It invades. A Primal scream that sings to my chest and deforms it. It feeds on me so that it can exist as a God I hate.

Bienaventurados sean los que se esfuerzan en existir
en lavar los pies del dios de la enfermedad
Contra qué pared hemos caído
En qué pared hemos escrito los nombres de
nuestra enfermedad
una madrugada cualquiera
quizá de junio mientras
dormimos sentados en la cama
y no podemos ver
el amor de la mujer y su niño
que recoge del piso a su marido borracho
y ni siquiera sabemos cómo preparar una Ocopa
y creemos que
la familia es la enemiga
después de vomitar sobre una bolsa
y sólo nos quedamos como fuera del tiempo

Inger, el cáncer ha llegado a la Tierra. Está dentro de la Tierra. Ha entregado su voz al enfermo.

Blessed be those who strive to exist
to wash the feet of the god of disease
Against which wall have we fallen
On which wall have we written the names of
our disease
some early morning
maybe in June while we
sleep sitting on the bed
and we cannot see
the love of the woman and her child
who picks up her drunken husband from the floor
and we don't even know how to make Ocopa
and we believe that
family is the enemy
after vomiting on a bag
and we just remain as if we were out of time

Inger, cancer has come to Earth. It is inside the Earth. It has given its voice to the diseased.

Mi cáncer dice:

tu pecho será vaciado y luego inflado con agua de mar. Tu joroba, tu aleta. Pero tu corazón como migaja de pan habrá esparcido su polvo enamorado en todos tus órganos.

En una Tierra de cemento, en montañas futuristas de rascacielos, sedimentado fondo revelado, que se detiene a través de transparentes ventanales, ingresa a la neblina como río de altura, manto tras manto de imperceptibles bordados milenarios, tan poco entendido, en la Tierra. Más liviano, ordenado, en una mística alquimia, desnuda.

My cancer says:
your chest will be emptied and then filled with seawater. Your hump back, your back fin. But your heart, like breadcrumbs, will have scattered its dust in love all over your organs.

On an earth of concrete, on futuristic mountains of skyscrapers, a sedimented unveiled background, stopping through transparent windows, entering the mist like a river up high, mantle after mantle of imperceptible millenary embroidery, so little understood, on Earth. Lighter, ordered, in a mystical alchemy, naked.

Abro el miedo. Es la enfermedad. Un caparazón creciendo dentro de otro caparazón para ser triturado.

Mi cáncer era algo que venía, tuvo nacimiento y tiene nacimiento, sigue viniendo hasta que respira. Como branquia, erizo y salamandra. Como talismán y sal. Como abandonado fósil, estalactita, pintura rupestre. Encuentra mi cuerpo perfecto. Lo toma vigorosamente en un deseo de violentar lo débil para que despierte.

Opening fear. It is the disease. A shell growing inside another shell in order to be crushed.

My cancer was something that had to come, it has been born, and it will be born, it keeps on coming until it takes a breath. Like a gill, a hedgehog , a salamander. Like a talisman and salt. Like an abandoned fossil, stalactite, cave painting. Finding my perfect body. Taking it vigorously in a desire to violate what is weak in order to awaken it.

Y teníamos que ser
aunque el caparazón de la apariencia
naciera antes que nosotros
Nuestra madre
rezaba a la virgen de Chapi y la muerte que
siempre quisimos que viniera por nosotros
finalmente ha venido
un deseo   un
deseo de una adolescente   una
madrugada cualquiera bajo
la muerte que recoge todos los días las almas
con mucha regularidad

El cáncer como un desorden creado de cúmulo y miedo para nombrar. Un significante confundido. Los vidriosos ojos fijos del cáncer de los pies manchados con barro que entregan frutos y más frutos y después cielo.

And we had to be
even if the shell of appearance
was born ahead of us
Our mother
prayed to the virgin of Chapi and the death that
we always wanted to come for us
has finally come
a wish   the
wish of a teenage girl   on
any given early morning under
death which collects souls every day
with great regularity

Cancer as a disorder created out of cumulus and fear of naming. A confused signifier. The glassy fixed eyes of cancer of the feet stained with mud-stained feet that deliver fruit and more fruit and then heaven.

Mi cáncer dice:

Teresa, la imagen difusa de lo que es. No hay fósforo oculto para prender, no hay rabia ni clavos, tampoco más allá. La que tienes adentro tira su juguete mental para que te pierdas. Alimento de invierno para el que dice No. Alimento para los que no saben soltar la estera. Alimento para los que repiten: celda y tú.

Inger, es el cáncer del agua que se eleva. Se eleva. Todos los siglos que tomaron las alas de los pájaros en formarse. Antes y después de que la primera enfermedad fuese pronunciada. Se trasciende. Diez veces. Mil veces. Señal invisible de la vida. No hay verdad ni mentira.

My cancer says:
Teresa, the fuzzy image of what is. There is no hidden matchstick to ignite, no rage, no nails, no afterlife either. The one within you throws her mental toy for you to lose yourself. Winter food for those who say No. Food for those who don't know how to let go of the strawmat. Food for those who repeat a jail cell and you.

Inger, it is the cancer of water rising. It rises. All the centuries it took for the wings of birds to form. Before and after the first disease was pronounced. It trascends itself. Ten times. A thousand times. Invisible sign of life. There is no truth or lie.

Abro el miedo. Como si alguien en medio de millones de lámparas encendidas apartara una. A treinta y nueve años luz apareció un nuevo sistema solar semejante al nuestro. El Tratado del Cielo en el sonido de una campana como el ruido que hacen los planetas y sus cuerpos. Tu primer grito como recién nacida. Nunca hubo silencio. A través de los números conocíamos lo real. Donde los martillos del herrero se tocan una música y un orden. Un peso. Desaparece una divinidad. Como si escucharas una vez más a tu madre embarazada tararear ese vals que dice tu voz existe mientras teje un roponcito de cuerdas. Hasta que tú cumples cuarenta años. Te enfermas. Tu esposo al año siguiente también se enferma y se quedan juntos como dos ropas viejas llenas de polvo. Como tu hermana que te dice que el amor para la familia no existe si no hay convivencia y habla y habla de sí misma hasta volverse un punto negro en la prosa que escribes. Cuando te abruma pensar que el sistema barre lo que ya no sirve y que entre lo que no sirve no sólo están las cosas sino tú y tu esposo y tu madre. Todos los enfermos del mundo.

Cuando el cáncer del trabajo pueda volar, mi enfermedad o mi salud serán. Cuando el cáncer del poeta pueda volar el cáncer será olvidado por todos. Y algo. Algo será.

Opening fear. As if someone amid millions of lighted lamps pushed one of them away. Thirty-nine light years away, a new solar system similar to ours appeared. The Treatise of Heaven within the sound of a bell like the noise made by planets and their bodies. Your first cry as a newborn. There was never any silence. Through the numbers, we knew what was real. Where the blacksmith's hammers touch each other, music and order. A weight. A divinity disappears. As if once again you listened to your pregnant mother humming that waltz that says your voice exists, as she weaves a small gown made of strings. Until you turn forty. You become ill. Your husband also gets sick the following year, and you stay together like two old pieces of clothing full of dust. Like your sister who tells you that love for your family wouldn't exist if it wasn't for cohabitation and she talks and talks about herself until she becomes a black spot in the prose you write. When you are overwhelmed to think that the system sweeps away what is no longer useful and that among what is no longer useful not only are there things but you and your husband and your mother. All the sick people in the world.

When the cancer of work can fly, my illness or my health will be. When the poet's cancer can fly, cancer will be forgotten by all. And something. Something will be.

Operados los cuerpos
en fila india
esperan la pastilla de la salvación
No hay resplandor
ni máquina para curar las amputaciones
Sólo celdas
siendo siempre
que algunos de los pobladores de Yungay
donde el aluvión enterró la ciudad han
salido a marchar contra la muerte
muertes que en los últimos años
han sido numerosas
en el continente sudamericano
donde solitarios indígenas de sus múltiples culturas
han perdido la memoria
sin que puedan dejar de dibujar imágenes
que ya no entienden o
que han mezclado además con símbolos
de la civilización de la barbarie
hasta desaparecer en estos países
inventados de nombres sin sentido
y realidad maravillosa
de Cien años de soledad
Aquí subo yo al Uraj Pacha
al mundo de los de arriba
de los envueltos en las pancas del capitalismo
como semillas de la pobreza eterna
lanzo ángeles

Mientras tanto el cáncer de la vejez avanza como un ejército, se manifiesta. Cruza el semáforo en rojo, el semáforo en verde. El cáncer del pensamiento nace, alumbra, contempla, se detiene, se pierde. Nos encuentra. La vitalidad es un recuerdo de la vitalidad, apariencia.

Operated bodies
in single file
waiting for the pill of salvation
There is no shining
no machine to cure the amputations
Only cells
always being
and some of the residents of Yungay
where the flood buried the city have
come out to march against death
deaths that in the last years
have been numerous
in the South American continent
where lonesome indigenous people of multiple cultures
have lost their memory
without being able to stop drawing images
that they no longer understand or
that they have also mixed with symbols
of the civilization of brutality
until disappearing in these countries
made up of senseless names
and a marvelous reality
of One Hundred Years of Solitude
Here I ascend to the Uraj pacha
to the world of those above
those wrapped in the cornhusks of capitalism
like the seeds of eternal poverty
casting angels

Meanwhile, the cancer of old age advances like an army, it manifests itself. It crosses the red light, the green light. The cancer of thought is born, illuminates, contemplates, stops, loses itself. It finds us. Vitality is a memory of vitality, appearance.

Mi cáncer dice:
El capitalismo se rompe como el pan y en un día cualquiera,
todos los miedos de la tierra se tocan.

Las cáscaras de los huevos caídos de algún árbol dicen que hubo un nido, una cría. O la apariencia es y las crías están enterradas bajo las hojas, la apariencia tocada por la apariencia, circunstancial amanecer contra una vitalidad extraña en lugar de algo, olvidar lo que está en el pasado. Antes. Antes. En este antes.

My cancer says:
Capitalism breaks like bread and on any given day, all fears on earth are touched.

The eggshells fallen from some tree saying there was a nest, a hatchling. Or appearance is and the hatchlings are buried under the leaves, appearance touched by appearance, circumstantial dawn against a strange vitality instead of something, forgetting what is in the past. Before. Before. In this before.

Abro el miedo. Es una joroba. Soy la niña que cubre su cabeza con una caja de cartón y pregunta: ¿estoy bonita, papá?

En lo siguiente, el cáncer de la luz se reconoce como un ciempiés que se adelanta y retrocede. Garúa, lluvia, paraguas, ocultan el sinsentido. Este jardín que ya nadie reconoce, de cáscara sin cría, de vitalidad sin vitalidad y de apariencia de la apariencia, ese algo, este cáncer quechua que fue grabado para no desaparecer. La historia lo esconde. Es puesto en un museo donde el cáncer del dónde estabas tú dice no.

Opening fear. It is a hump. I am the little girl who covers her head with a cardboard box and asks: am I pretty, daddy?

From then on, the cancer of light is recognized as a centipede that moves forward and backward. Drizzle, rain, umbrellas, hiding the nonsense. This garden that no one recognizes anymore, a shell with no hatchling, of vitality without vitality, of the appearance of appearance, that something, this Quechua cancer that was engraved so as not to disappear. History hides it. It is placed in a museum where the cancer of 'where were you' says no.

El temor y la belleza existen
El movimiento la potencia de la que venimos existe
una filigrana cubriéndonos los ojos un punto en la Nada
un asterisco una carta a todos los seres humanos para que entiendan que
el agua vence al oro

y mientras todo el Perú se inunda en un clima desconocido
una mujer emerge del barro junto a un toro y un cerdo una equivalencia
de la naturaleza un la
la se escucha en el oído atrofiado de un anciano
como si la música se redujera a esa única nota cuando ya hemos vivido
lo suficiente
y sólo pudiésemos percibir la microscópica respiración de las bacterias
microscópica como la danza de los parásitos en nuestra sangre
y las vibraciones de nuestros glóbulos rojos,
como el paso lento de los invertebrados tardígrados
como los granos presolares de los meteoritos
como la soledad del electrón en el hidrógeno
¿qué hago con estas piedras?

El cáncer de la fragilidad se esconde. En una fotografía mojada las caras de mis
hermanos se deforman.

Fear and beauty exist
The movement the potential from which we come from exists
a filigree covering our eyes a dot within Nothingness
an asterisk a letter to all human beings so that they may understand that
water defeats gold

and while all of Peru is flooded in an unknown weather
a woman emerges from the mud next to a bull and a pig an equivalence
of nature an A chord
A is heard in the atrophied ear of an old man
as if music were reduced to that single note when we have lived
long enough
and we could only perceive the microscopic breathing of bacteria
microscopic like the dance of parasites in our blood
and the vibrations of our red blood cells,
like the slow pace of invertebrate tardigrades
like the pre-solar grains of meteorites
like the loneliness of an electron in hydrogen
what am I to do with these stones?

The cancer of fragility hides. In a wet photograph, the faces of my siblings are deformed.

Mi cáncer dice:

vivo en el valle del Solo. Conozco el sueño de la Tierra. Soy más antiguo que la luna. Estuve en el principio cuando fue la palabra. Aprendí el relato de todas las moléculas de este mundo. Por eso, tus células hablan conmigo. Me cuentan sobre ti. Yo conocí a la primera mujer. Veo algo de ella en tus ojos. No temas. Hace siglos que reconozco el olor de los cadáveres. Tú no vas a morir.

Se mezclan las vidas y las cosas del mundo debajo del mar y se vuelve una amalgama de fragmentos de mi memoria. Flotan. Se hunden. Y avanzan. Unas sobre otras. De manera caótica. Encallan en mi cuerpo. Lo toman y lo trasforman, un laberinto. Una vocal pronunciada por el loro.

My cancer says:

I live in the Solo Valley. I know the dream of the Earth. I am older than the moon. I was in the beginning as was the word. I learned the tale of all the molecules of this world. That is why your cells talk to me. They tell me about you. I met the first woman. I see something of her in your eyes. Don't be afraid. I have recognized the smell of corpses for centuries. You are not going to die.

The lives and things of the world are mixed up under the sea and become an amalgam of fragments of my memory. They float. They sink. And they advance. One on top of the other. In a chaotic way. They run ashore in my body. They take it and transform it into a labyrinth. A vowel pronounced by a parrot.

Abro el miedo. Mi cáncer escucha el silencio de mis órganos. Los hilos negros de la calma. Pregunto a mi cáncer. A ese Dios melancólico y persistente que me taladra. La espera de su respuesta me deja ver que las cosas no pesan. Ánimo. Crema de cúrcuma y agua de repollo para el dolor. Todos se van y yo me quedo. En mi cuarto atiende una enfermera migrante. Mi cáncer sigue escuchando atentamente el silencio de mis órganos. La enfermera escribe en su cuaderno: cuerpo mojado, leche de madre, da la espalda. Mi cáncer me mira a la distancia. Sonríe y sigue su camino hacia la ciudad de las enfermedades. Las batas blancas y las ambulancias transportan el sonido de la libélula. La ciudad de las enfermedades contiene al amor de madre y su violencia. Junto a mi cama, en un frasco de vidrio, el lloro de los virtuosos y de los piadosos. Las cosas se terminan como nosotros. A lo lejos, la caja de inyecciones como un juguete extraviado.

El cáncer del corazón se calla y descansa. Una cultura sumergida. Un cáncer inventado. El que viene de otro cáncer. El primero. El último. El que existe. El que todavía. El que estás incubando. El que estás escribiendo. El que aún no se nombra. El cáncer de todos los cánceres. El del esfuerzo humano. El del silencio. Encuentra mi cuerpo. Toma un órgano que toma otros órganos. Sostiene mi pulmón. Lo mece con sus brazos incompletos.

Opening fear. My cancer listens to the silence of my organs. The black threads of calm. I ask my cancer. That melancholic and persistent God that drills me. The wait for his response allows me to see that things are weightless. Cheer up. Turmeric cream and cabbage water for the pain. Everyone leaves and I stay. A migrant nurse attends to my room. My cancer is still listening closely to the silence of my organs. The nurse writes in her notebook: wet body, mother's milk, turns her back. My cancer looks at me from a distance. It smiles and continues its way to the city of diseases. The white robes and ambulances carry the sound of the dragonfly. The city of diseases contains a mother's love and her violence. By my bedside, in a glass jar, the weeping of the virtuous and the pious. Things end as we do. From afar, the box of injections is like a lost toy.

The cancer of the heart falls silent and rests. A submerged culture. A made-up cancer. The one that comes from another cancer. The first one. The last one. The one that exists. The one that still. The one you are incubating. The one you are writing. The one that is still unnamed. The cancer of all cancers. That of human endeavor. That of silence. It finds my body. It takes an organ that takes other organs. It holds my lung. It rocks it with its incomplete arms.

Inger, ¿sabías que los quipus existen?

los quipus existen
son marcas silenciosas
sosteniendo los órganos de una cultura sumergida
el mono titi y el hombre de Chivateros
las gardenias existen girasoles Gianuzzi

y el hostal el ají amarillo
sobre todas las cosas existen también los totorales de Huanchaco
las tortugas gigantes de Galápagos existen únicas durmientes y aburridas
en una isla de únicos durmientes y aburridos existen
longevidad evolutiva
y los muñecos piratas de peluche de King Kong de Polvos Azules
de Polvos Rosados de Polvos Morados existe si existen los Polvos Azules
si el ají amarillo en Polvos Azules existe el ají amarillo
sobre todas las cosas existe sobre todas las cosas donde existe el hambre de
los ricos sobre todas las cosas donde existe la justicia
de los indios como paz como rabia como paz molida
en el batán milenario el mate-Gianuzzi el ají amarillo
sobre todas las cosas por supuesto que existirá por supuesto
que existiremos el ají amarillo que comemos existe
Pachacamac Paracas existen y la Biblioteca de Babel de Borges
junto al Axolotel de Cortázar Garabombo el invisible escondido
tras su miseria con muchos otros existirá, Ino Moxo existe
y la muñeca Chancay como el color anaranjado
del ají amarillo
y tallada en la piedra de los doce ángulos la lágrima de la última
princesa inca la rana semejante a la soga y en lo más suave
de la soga la dulzura plegada vieja
como mis orejas por entre la lengua húmeda de mi esposo esta belleza
desenfocada trinitaria que envuelve a los recién nacidos donde come
un caníbal que ha perdido la memoria existen los miles de ismos
destruidos tu hocico salivoso como mis pies
y Túpac Amaru Túpac Amaru descuartizado existe

70

Inger, did you know that quipus exist?

quipus exist
they are silent marks
sustaining the organs of a submerged culture
the Titi monkey and the Chivateros man
gardenias Gianruzzi sunflowers exists

and the aji amarillo colored hostel
above all things, the totora reeds of Huanchaco also exist
the Galapagos giant tortoises exist the only ones bored and sleeping
on an island of bored and sleeping ones exist
evolutionary longevity
and the counterfeit plush toys of King Kong in Polvos Azules
in Polvos Rosados in Polvos Morados exist if Polvos Azules exists
if the aji amarillo in Polvos Azules exists the aji amarillo
above all things exists above all things where the hunger of
the rich exists above all things where the justice
of the indians exists as peace as rage as minced peace
in the millenary batan stone the Gianuzzi mate the aji amarillo pepper
above all things of course it will exist of course
we will exist the aji amarillo we eat exists
Pachacamac Paracas exist and Borges' Library of Babel
next to Cortázar's Axolotl Garabombo the invisible hidden
behind his misery with many others will exist, Ino Moxo exists
and the Chancay doll as the orange color
of aji amarillo
and carved in the twelve-angled stone the tears of the last
Incan princess the frog similar to the rope and in the softest part
of the rope the old, folded sweetness
like my ears in between my husband's wet tongue this beauty
unfocused and trinitarian that wraps the newborns where
a cannibal who has lost his memory eats and the thousands of isms exist
destroyed your salivating snout like my feet
and Túpac Amaru Túpac Amaru dismembered exists

Túpac Amaru amarrado a su camisa de fuerza
existe Túpac Amaru lloroso como un niño
existe Túpac Amaru sentado sobre el río Canta
donde la muerte lava la ropa y los zapatos de los muertos
los héroes las víctimas existen los uniformes de los héroes junto a
los clítoris cortados de las niñas de Emberá
las mujeres esterilizadas del Fujimorismo
las paredes de madera de una fabela y los besos
existen los seguidores de Túpac Amaru mestizos como el oído
del que sabe escuchar todos los sonidos por supuesto que existirán
por supuesto que existiremos y el ají amarillo bajo el cuchillo del ají amarillo
como el disco de Newton existiremos como aurora boreal existiremos
como el ruido de las finas gotas de agua
de mi lavadero malogrado del viento en las raíces
del ciprés octogenario
existiremos
como las sillas voladoras empolvadas del juego
mecánico de un parque,
como la tuberculosis de María que no se pudo curar quizá como
el nombre raro de Chivi
quizá como la hoja de la espinaca acelga unos granos de café
prensados en el viejo mundo pero el huevo
es la gallina decía mi abuela el huevo del viejo mundo es la gallina
pero no la gallina torpe de la que hablaba Lispector
si es que existe Lispector gallina es gallina
dice mi abuela el huevo es la gallina pero no
la gallina verde que pintó el artesano de Ayacucho
cuando todas las cosas eran de barro y tenían ojos tan gallinas
en su origen
el huevo es más gallina los nidos desaparecen cuando lo mira el perro.

El cáncer del ir a buscar. El de las manos llenas. Es mi madre. Es mi padre. Es un tubérculo en mi ovario derecho, en mi ovario izquierdo. Un cometa incrustado en mis ojos como un vidrio universal.

Tupac Amaru tied to his straitjacket
Túpac Amaru exists crying like a child
Túpac Amaru exists seated on the Canta River
where death washes the clothes and shoes of the dead
the heroes the victims exist the uniforms of heroes next to
the severed clitorises of Emberá girls
the sterilized women of Fujimorism
the wooden walls of a fabela and kisses
exist the followers of Tupac Amaru mestizos like the ear
of one who knows how to listen to all sounds of course they will exist
of course we will exist and the aji amarillo under the knife of aji amarillo
like Newton's disc we will exist like the aurora borealis we shall exist
like the sound of fine water droplets
of my broken washboard of wind in the roots
of the octogenarian cypress
we will exist
like the dusty flying chairs of
a mechanical ride in a park,
like Maria's tuberculosis that could not be cured perhaps like
Chivi's weird name
perhaps like the leaf of spinach chard a few coffee beans
pressed in the old world but the egg
is the chicken my grandmother said the egg of the old world is the chicken
but not the clumsy chicken Lispector talked about
if Lispector exists then a chicken is a chicken
my grandmother says the egg is the chicken but not
the green chicken painted by the artisan from Ayacucho
when all things were made of clay and had such chicken eyes
in their origin
the egg is more the chicken the nests disappear when the dog looks at it.

The cancer of fetching. That of full hands. It is my mother. It is my father. It is a tuber in my right ovary, in my left ovary. A comet embedded in my eyes like a universal glass.

Mi cáncer dice:
Busca entre la canasta de los huevos de la gallina y escucha
este mensaje: levántate de esa cama, esa jaula de tela. Mira a
los ojos a tu esposo, el que sigue contigo y deja que todas las
cosas buenas que están dentro de ti pasen a sus ojos. Dile al
oído: yo soy tu familia. Deja de tener miedo pena angustia.
Cree: hay suficiente. Ten por primera vez en tu vida: paz.
Escucha lo que existe.

*El cáncer del fracaso de la lengua. El de la tela sin fin. El que no sabe traer el
mundo. Extinción. Dentro del ajedrez de la naturaleza donde todos somos
peones de lo mismo.*

My cancer says:
Look through the basket of hen's eggs and listen to this message: get up from that bed, that cage made of fabric. Look into the eyes of your husband, the one who is still with you, and let all the good things that are inside of you pass through his eyes. Whisper in his ear: I am your family. Stop being afraid of fear, sorrow, anguish. Believe: there is enough. Have for the first time in your life: peace. Listen to what exists.

The cancer of the failure of language. That of endless fabric. That which does not know how to bring about the world. Extinction. Inside the chessboard of nature where we are all pawns of the same game.

HERIDA / WOUND

Derrumbada la torre de Babel existe y
el once de septiembre existe
los incendiados de la guerra con Chile como limbos descoloridos
y también los seis estudiantes asesinados y los cuarenta y tres desaparecidos
de Ayotzinapa
como cuando
el ronquido de los que están bajo tierra
nos despierta alarmados por el futuro de nuestros hijos
una guerra como
pintada con nuestras orejas nuestras piernas, nuestros brazos un tiro
sobre nuestras cabezas atravesando los siglos y la cara
paralizada del herido el herido entregado por su patria
para ser herido existen colonias e ilegítimos que
no saben que son ilegítimos existen la marinera y
las prosas apátridas
existe toda la prole de Francisco Pizarro
la piedra absoluta de Martín Adán y la mesa donde escribo
Haz contado todo y no es suficiente

El cáncer de las invocaciones ha vuelto sobre sí mismo. Ha visto su rostro sobre el lago. Se ha asustado con su reflejo y se ha escondido en el bosque de las niñas que golpean la mesa para que se caiga la carne. Ha rayado el arenal y ha soplado su nombre. Se ha preguntado sobre la claridad y no ha encontrado respuesta. Ha regresado para descifrarla. A veces con temor.

Collapsed the tower of Babel exists and
September Eleventh exists
the burnt ones of the war with Chile as discolored limbos
also the six murdered and the forty-three missing students
in Ayotzinapa
as when
the snoring of those who are buried underground
wakes us up alarmed for the future of our children
as if a war were
painted with our ears our legs, our arms a shot
above our heads crossing the centuries and the paralyzed
face of the wounded the wounded man giving himself to his homeland
to be wounded the colonies exist and illegitimate sons who
do not know they are illegitimate the Marinera dance and
the Stateless Prose exist
all the offspring of Francisco Pizarro exists
the absolute stone of Martín Adán and the table where I write
You have accounted for everything and it is not enough

The cancer of invocations has turned back on itself. Has seen its face on the lake. It has been frightened by its reflection and has hidden in the forest of those girls who bang on the table to make the meat fall off. It has broken the desert wilderness and blown out its name. It has wondered about the clarity and has not found an answer. It has returned to decipher it. Sometimes in fear.

Mi cáncer dice:
tu pecho que fue tuyo y ahora es mío quedó enredado con el
pabilo de mi corazón

Al fin le hemos visto las manos asomarse y acariciar las nubes, el pasto, las cuevas, los relámpagos, el sexo. Al fin se ha reunido con su materia más allá del miedo. Parcialmente olvidada.

My cancer says:
your breast that was yours and is now mine was entangled with
the wick of my heart.

*At last, we have seen its hands reach out and caress the clouds, the grass, the
caves, the lightning, the sex. At last, it has been reunited with its matter beyond
fear. Partially forgotten.*

El amor no se asusta

El amor no se esconde del sollozo
lo abraza firme como el creyente al santo
Por eso siempre ha sido tan milagrosa la imagen de
Chacalón
siempre la chicha triste como estampita de algún mapuche triste de
Ceferino
tan grandemente formada extensamente bautizada la triste comunión
de los que sobran
y siempre un ejército que arrea pueblos pueblos negros pueblos cobrizos
pueblos derecho de gentes autodefensa de los pueblos libres sobre los
pueblos prohibidos como decía un filósofo de un pueblo triste existen
sus oraciones sonámbulas preparan el cuchillo que corta la bondad
y las audiencias brutales que aplauden
la política sonora de la nada
existen un sol enterrado entre Comas y el desierto de Atacama
el adobe humedecido de Chan Chan tan geométrico y la red
envuelta envuelta como las palabras que no tienen raíz
en ninguna lengua

*Tan extraña como las pocas mujeres que pueden reconocer al hombre que llevan
adentro. Gobernadas por el hambre. Negándolo. Recuerdo de su hipocresía.
Calmando su realidad tartamuda. Enderezándola como a una célula recién
nacida.*

Love is not afraid

Love does not hide from sobbing
but embraces it firmly as the believer does the saint
That is why it has always been so miraculous the image of
Chacalón
always sad chicha music as the holy card of some Mapuche feeling sad for
Ceferino
so greatly formed extensively baptized the sad holy communion
of those who are left over
and always an army ploughing through peoples black people copper people
peoples right of the peoples self-defense of free peoples against
forbidden peoples as the philosopher of a sad people used to say exist
their somnambulist prayers preparing the knife that cuts kindness
and the brutal audiences that applaud
the resounding politics of nothingness
a sun buried between Comas and the Atacama Desert exists
the moistened mudbricks of Chan Chan so geometrical and the fishing net
entangled entangled like words which have no root
in any language

As strange as the few women who can recognize the man they carry inside.
Ruled by hunger. Denying it. Remembrance of their hypocrisy. Soothing their
stuttering reality. Straightening it like a newborn cell.

Mi cáncer dice:

Yo soy el que protege una cosa por debajo de otras para ti. Sé que estás cansada y sabes ya que sólo hay preguntas. No tengas miedo y di: sí. Y cambia cromo, culpa y pena reina de la morería. Sonríe, sonríe. Escucha lo que existe.

El cáncer de las invocaciones a pedido conciencia, una voz. Borramiento.

My cancer says:
I am the one who protects beneath others for you. I know you are tired and you know already that there are only questions. Do not be afraid and say: yes. And change chrome, guilt and sorrow queen of the Moorish lands. Smile, smile. Listen to what exists.

The cancer of invocations on demand conscience, a voice. Erasure.

La pregunta gobierna el mundo
existe como las culturas
borradas existen
como preguntas en la oscuridad
existen
como partículas que gobiernan el
mundo
de un tiempo a otro imposible
de medir
Inkarri midiendo
la partícula de Dios existe en su reino
imposible existe y sus hijos las estaciones del subdesarrollo
los miles de físicos sudamericanos que sueñan con hacer física
en Alemania
cines convertidos en iglesias evangélicas fanáticos y
eucaristías sin vino
sin monjas
ni curas ni papas entregados a la castidad
santas Marías Magdalenas sin Pedros ni Pablos
evangelizando hombres ni trinidades ni profetas
que anuncien o denuncien, ni bienaventurados de ninguna clase
y una imposición de manos sobre el cuerpo de alguien
de unos elegidos a los que su Jesús no les ha encomendado decir
el que esté en pecado entienda su pecado
sin espejos rotos en miles de pedazos que asemejan a un dios medieval
y ángeles
fragmentos desordenados que no pueden adorar la imagen completa de
la imagen
la imagen a la que los niños sin religión giran
como botellas borrachas
que no llevan ningún mensaje o evangelio la imagen de algún primerizo
que cree entender el ser de la jarra y las tumbas que sin
tangos ni huaynos
invisibles y occidentales existen con su polvo
y sus flores de plástico existen o las migraciones del polen

The question rules the world
it does exists as erased
cultures exist
as questions in the dark
exist
as particles that rule the
world
from time to time now impossible
to measure
Inkarri measuring
The God particle exists in its realm
impossible exists and its children the stations of underdevelopment
the thousands of South American physicists who dream of doing physics
in Germany
movie theaters converted into fanatical evangelical churches and
communions without wine
without nuns
neither priests nor popes devoted to chastity
holy Mary Magdalenes with no Paul or Peter
evangelizing men no trinities or prophets
announcing or denouncing, nor blessed ones of any kind
and an imposition of hands on someone's body
of some chosen ones to whom their Jesus has not entrusted them to say
let him who is in sin understand his sin
without mirrors broken into thousands of pieces resembinge a medieval god
and angels
disordered fragments that cannot adore the complete image of
the image
the image around which children without religion revolve
like in a game of spin the bottle
carrying no message or gospel the image of some first-timer
who thinks he understands the being of the jar and the tombs that without
tangos or huaynos
invisible and westerner exist with their dust
and their plastic flowers exist or the migrations of pollen

existen fieles
y lúcidas o el martillo la madera existen
y la costa del Pacífico con su mar hablándole al oído a un músico uruguayo
guanacos y guano la imagen completa de obreros de Construcción civil
proletarios y villeros de la treinta y uno existen la expresión horrible del
capital existe con o sin Trump
María Helena Moyano y Pedro Huilca Flores Galindo y Arguedas
existen sin zonas urbanas ni condominios ni torres existen
con marchas de universitarios de Argentina, marchas de universitarios
de Chile, con o sin policías
existen con Bachelet Vizcarra o Macri permutaciones transposiciones
distorsiones de los auténticos padres

Resistir. El cáncer de la memoria es multiplicar. Tan solitaria como la probabilidad de lograr que exista algo. Tan claramente imperfecta, tan muerta, como sólo el perro vagabundo busca a su amo, su fidelidad a la sombra. Como si el cáncer de la memoria no fuese el cáncer del que se ha rendido en su demora.

they faithfully exist
and lucidly or the hammer and the wood exist
and the Pacific coast with its sea talking in the ear of an uruguayan musician
guanacos and guano the complete picture of Union Construction workers
the proletarians and slum dwellers of Barrio 31 exist the horrible expression
of capital exists with or without Trump
María Helena Moyano and Pedro Huilca Flores Galindo and Arguedas
exist without urban zones, condominiums or towers.
with university student marches in Argentina, university student marches
in Chile, with or without the police
exist with Bachelet Vizcarra or Macri permutations transpositions
distortions of the authentic fathers

To resist. The cancer of memory is to multiply. As solitary as the probability of achieving the existence of something. As clearly imperfect, as dead, as only the stray dog seeking for his master, his fidelity to the shadow. As if the cancer of memory were not the cancer of the one who has given up in its delay.

Mi cáncer dice:
En el museo de la paz el selkman aún vive cantando fuera del tiempo.

El cáncer del ojo de vidrio enfrentado a la claridad de contar del cáncer del ojo abierto. En la emoción de la que nacen sus palabras, en las cartas perdidas entre el lenguaje y el corazón, en ellas se entrega la plenitud, se releva la cordura, se despliegan existencias, cacharros, mensajes y heridas, enmarcan sus temblores y queman el azar, el destino. Salvan porque salvan, o porque la fe se mantiene incondicional, consuela y protege la propia felicidad de nuestras gargantas. Como si el cáncer del hambre te ayudara a entender el secreto de tu biología.

My cancer says:
In the peace museum, the Selk`nam still lives singing out of time.

The cancer of the glass eye is confronted with the clarity of telling the cancer of the glass eye. In the emotion from which words are born, in the lost letters between the language and the heart, in them wholesomeness is delivered, sanity is relieved, existence unfolds, junk, messages and wounds, framing their tremors and burning chance, destiny. They save because they save, or because faith remains unconditional, consoles and protects the very happiness of our throats. As if the cancer of hunger would help you understand the secret of your biology.

Los vencidos existen
La culpa existe
y todas las guerras del mundo
entre las grandes plazas de las ciudades del mundo
las bombas explotan como la gran odisea del dolor

Uchuraccay el penal de Lurigancho

Uchuraccay 26
de enero de 1983

Lurigancho 4
de octubre de 1985

8 periodistas, un guía y un comunero
muertos en Uchuraccay

35 presos quemados en el pabellón
Británico de Lurigancho

el pasador solitario de un zapato la vida inocente
esparcida por el piso de un campo
por el piso de escombros de una cárcel fría

el odio existe el odio existe
tan enfocado como el voto ciego del pobre como
la derecha militarista de un país pobre
y aun así cada nuevo siglo
el joven estudiante no deja de marchar
pero se vuelve adulto y entonces quiere
quiere de todo una casa dos tres autos viajar por el mundo
y ya no quiere recordar
que su padre vino del campo
que su madre vino del río
que sus antepasados fueron indios

The defeated exist
Guilt exists
and all the wars of the world
among the great squares of the cities of the world
bombs explode as in a great odyssey of pain

Uchuraccay Lurigancho prison

Uchuraccay 26th
of January, 1983

Lurigancho 4th
of october, 1985

8 journalists, a tour guide and a community member
found dead in Uchuraccay

35 prisoners burnt in
Lurigancho's British Pavilion

the solitary lace of a shoe the innocent life
scattered across the ground on a field
across the rubble floor of a cold prison

hate exists hate exists
as focused as the blind vote of the poor as
the militaristic right wing of a poor country
and yet every new century
the young student does not stop marching
but he becomes an adult and then he wants
wants everything one house two three cars to travel the world
and no longer wants to remember
that his father came from the country
that his mother came from the river
that his ancestors were indians

fueron negros esclavos
traficados
gentes sin derechos puestos a un lado por la Historia pueblos
sin derechos puestos a un lado por la Iglesia, países sin derechos
puestos a un lado por sus dueños continentes sin derechos
puestos a un lado por unas cuantas familias ricas de este mundo
y así como una tragedia como una comedia
el odio crece como una maraña negra de pelos y vuelve a comenzar

Los huevos del cáncer metafísico se rompen. Lo inabarcable extiende sus colores como manteles sobre las mesas. Compone obras de paja.

were black slaves
trafficked
folks with no rights pushed aside by History peoples
with no rights pushed aside by the Church, countries with no rights
pushed aside by their owners continents with no rights
pushed aside by a few rich families of this world
and so like a tragedy like a comedy
hate grows like a black tangle of hairs and starts all over again

The eggs of the metaphysical cancer break. The unfathomable spreads its colors like tablecloths on the tables. It composes works of straw.

Mi cáncer dice:

Tu lucha está dentro de la poesía como un pequeño huevo. En ella no hay odio. Torpe como la gallina viniste a mí, lenta como la infancia. La balanza rompió. De tu telaraña manaba mi temor. ¿Qué olor tenías? Tu búsqueda era implacable. Todo el paraíso reducido a una ancha línea roja. Del principio al fin de la Historia.

El cáncer del consumo abre su tienda. Se vende. Deja caer su monedero. Niega el discurso, el sentido. Se inauguran los hospitales, los cuerpos que ya no importan. El capital es una vitrina que te atrapa. Los enfermos miran tras la ventana de la vanidad. Su imaginación converge con el desgaste.

My cancer says:

Your battle is within poetry like a little egg. There is no hate within it. Clumsy as a chicken you came to me, slow as childhood. The scale broke. From your web, my fear flowed. What scent did you have? Your search was relentless. All of paradise reduced to a thick red line. From the beginning to the end of History.

The cancer of consumption opens its store. It is for sale. It drops its wallet. It denies the discourse, the meaning. Hospitals are inaugurated, the bodies that no longer matter. Capital is a showcase that traps you. The diseased look behind the window of vanity. Their imagination converges with the wear and tear.

América también existe
América existe
Inger, no nos niegues

América existe
el aymara existe; y la flor de papa, la flor de papa
y el quechua existen; y Resígaro, Resígaro
las alpacas existen; Resígaro, aire;
y quinuales existen; las alpacas existen;
alpacas, abarema, aiphanes, arterias
los ronsocos existen; los mayas, las llicllas
los orejones existen; los ronsocos, los ronsocos
yana wayra, la momia Juanita y los intis; los intis
existen; los intis la chicha de jora; y los mitos
existen; los mitos, los intis, la chicha de jora
anata existe; la furia y la fiesta
existen; y el Señor de Muruhuay; Rosa de Lima,
los huérfanos y la vizcacha existen; los suyos
existen, la fragilidad; la fuerza de la fragilidad;
y la oscuridad plena existe, el sauce y el sauco
existen, y brunellia, la mezcla, la indiferencia
existen; y el cebú y el pejesapo existen,
y el petróleo de Venezuela existe, y las causas, las causas
el ukuku existe, con su hielo amarrado a la espalda
existe, con su danza protectora
y su devoción para el Señor de Q'oyllur Riti existe; alegre
existe; en Paucartambo y Quispicanchi y en la montaña nevada;
también los perros existen; y el gallinazo carroñero, el
      cóndor andino
el buitre; las bromelias y la soledad del oso melero;
los khipu kamayuq existen y lianas existen;
las verdades existen, las intensas, las católicas,
las éticas; el acelerador de partículas Ciclotrón existe
y la cucaracha blanca;

The Americas also exists
The Americas exist
Inger, do not deny us

The Americas exists
aymara exists; and the potato flower, the potato flower
and quechua exist; and Resígaro, Resígaro
alpacas exist; Resígaro, air;
and quinua fields exist; alpacas exist;
alpacas, abarema, aiphanes, arteries
capybaras exist; the mayans, the llicllas
the orejones exist; the capybaras, the capybaras
yana wayra, Mummy Juanita and the intis; the intis
exist; the intis the chicha de jora; and the myths
exist; the myths, the intis, the chicha de jora
anata exists; the feast and the fury
exist; and the Lord of Muruhuay; Rose of Lima,
the orphans and the vizcacha exist; the suyos
exist, the fragility; the strength of fragility;
and the full darkness exists, the willow and the elder tree
exist, and brunellia, the mixture, the indifference
exist; and the zebu and the pejesapo exist,
and the oil of Venezuela exists, and the causes, the causes
the ukuku exists, with his ice strapped to the back
exists, with his protective dance
and his devotion to the Lord of Q'oyllur Riti exists; joyful
exists; in Paucartambo and Quispicanchi and in the snowy mountain;
the dogs also exist; and the carrion-eating buzzard, the
      Andean condor
the vulture; the bromeliads and the solitude of the honey bear;
the khipu kamayuq exist and lianas exist;
the truths exist, the intense, the catholic,
the ethical ones; the Cyclotron particle accelerator exists
and the white cockroach;

y las flores carnívoras existen y el gracioso caminar sobre los ríos del
Amazonas del lagarto Jesucristo donde
los pajareros existen, los pajareros existen
en selvas donde la gente esculpe sirenas sobre la madera
que no conoce la nieve con la que juegan los niños de Alaska.

El cáncer de la necesidad es un gigante. Aplasta las chozas de los pobres. Aplasta las faldas voladoras de las mujeres. Aplasta. Los ciudadanos no existen.

and the carnivorous flowers exist and the graceful walking on the rivers of
the Amazon of the lizard Jesus Christ where
the birdcatchers exist, the birdcatchers exist
in jungles where the people sculpt mermaids on wood
who don't know the snow that Alaskan children play with.

*The cancer of need is a giant. It crushes the shacks of the poor. It crushes
the flying skirts of women. It crushes. The citizens do not exist.*

Mi cáncer dice:

aquí también estás tú. Eres una niña que no sabe divertirse. Tus tímpanos crecen después de tu primera muerte. Escuchas la partida de tu padre. Juegas con tu sinceridad como si fuese una muñeca y con tu desastre como si fuese una cometa. La poesía curará tu cuerpo y el de tu padre. Se lavarán las culpas.

El cáncer de la alegría es rojo. La ameba se desliza en sus pies falsos. No hay bien que sea real.

My cancer says:
here you are too. You're a little girl who doesn't know how to have fun. Your eardrums grow after your first death. You hear your father's departure. You play with your sincerity as if it were a doll and with your disaster as if it were a kite. Poetry will heal your body and your father's body. Guilt will be washed away.

The cancer of joy is red. The amoeba slithers on its false feet. There is no good that is real.

La poesía existe como el primer animal
El racismo existe, los barrios, la memoria

e ichu y manzanas y conejos y floripondios,
la tristeza existe, el racismo existe;

las ruinas existen, los turistas que las visitan
existen y la fotografía de las ruinas

piedras de ruinas milenarias sin nombre existen,
piedras de ruinas que se llaman Caral, Chichén Itzá,
Teotihuacán existen y los miles de huacos retratos

existen, en la historia imperial de los caídos; existe
también la emoción, y la maca y Pachacamac existen,
los terroristas, el minero peruano, los hijos del minero peruano;

y los ronderos campesinos existen, una callada aldea,
sentenciado, seco y quemado a metrallazos,
los ronderos campesinos existen; a oscuras
desaparecidos existen los ronderos campesinos,
con sus ponchos, sus polleras, con su mirada petrificada existen

los ronderos campesinos, y los apus existen, enormes
como señores temibles, los manantiales existen;
los manantiales, cristalinos, celestes y dulces,
del misterio, extinguidos,
este aliento de hambre, negro, que está esfumándose

Algo parecido a una jaula cae sobre nosotros. Es el cáncer de la tristeza.

Poetry exists as the first animal
Racism exists, neighborhoods, memory exists

and ichu and apples and rabbits and angel's trumpets
sadness exists, racism exists;

ruins exist, the tourists who visit them
exist and the photographs of the ruins

stones of millenary ruins with no name exist,
stones of ruins that are called Caral, Chichen Itza,
Teotihuacan exist and the thousands of huaco portraits

exist, in the imperial history of the fallen; exists
also the emotion, and the maca and Pachacamac exist,
the terrorists, the Peruvian miners, the sons of the Peruvian miners;

and the rondas campesinas exist, a silent village,
sentenced, twisted and turned by shrapnel,
the peasant ronderos exist; in the dark
disappeared the peasant ronderos exist,
with their ponchos, their polleras, with their petrified gaze exist,

the peasant ronderos, and the apus exist, enormous
as fearsome overlords, the water springs exist;
the water springs, crystalline, celestial and sweet,
of the mystery, extinguished,
this breath of hunger, black, that is vanishing

Something similar to a cage falls upon us. It is the cancer of sadness.

Mi cáncer dice:

tu memoria es hundimiento sin unidad ni coherencia. Por ello, un corazón recurre a otro corazón para curarse. Aprende de la que oró al silencio y en voz alta reclámale golpeando a tu pecho ausente tres veces: yo confieso, yo ruego y acepto: por ninguna culpa, por ninguna culpa, por ninguna gravísima culpa te he perdido.

Háblale a lo que existe.

Evoco. Abro un agujero en mi célula inmortal y le enseño a morir. Salgo a ver el destello de la que veré por última vez. Saco las sábanas de mi cama y limpio las manchas de sangre de mi colchón. Ilumino.

My cancer says:

your memory is a sinking without unity or coherence. For this reason, a heart turns to another heart for healing. Learn from the one who prayed to silence and complain to her out loud while beating your absent chest three times: I confess, I beg and accept: through no fault of my own, through no fault of my own, through no grave fault of my own I have lost you.

Speak to what exists.

I evoke. I open a hole in my immortal cell and I teach it how to die. I go out to see the glimmer of the one I will see for the last time. I pull the sheets off my bed and I clean the blood stains on my mattress. I illuminate.

La cura existe, la cura existe
el bordado diminuto sobre el yute de mi abuela
Todo tan limpio como era en el principio

La paz existe
el humilde lavado de pies del papa Francisco a los doce presos de la
cárcel de Paliano
como bendición para el desamparado

un avatar como una encarnación de Dios

ya sea
que creas o
no, en cualquier hora
en que quizá como nunca
haz pensado que te pueden amar
en cualquier hora
quizá de febrero, mientras
lees Pedro Páramo de Juan Rulfo
y necesitas naufragar sobre una pregunta

contar la historia de la procesión de la papa
que pintó Gerardo Chávez sobre la humildad de los costales
con tierras de color que el mismo preparó, y que casi
perdiste tu ojo derecho a los cinco años
y jugar al Mundo
como si el camino al cielo
fuese el camino a la poesía.
y sólo hay un día para descansar
y percibir en silencio, mientras tu familia peregrina
hacia Ancón,
para lavar la ropa de tu abuela muerta como
purificación de su viaje y continúa
viviendo en cada uno de ustedes, mientras
Gerardo Chávez

The cure exists, the cure exists
the tiny embroidery on my grandmother's jute dress
Everything as clean as it was in the beginning

Peace exists
Pope Francis humbly washing the feet of twelve inmates
in Paliano Prison
like a blessing for the helpless

an avatar as an incarnation of God

whether
you believe or
not, at any hour
when perhaps as never before
you have thought you could be loved
at any hour
maybe in February, while
you read Pedro Páramo by Juan Rulfo
and you need to be shipwrecked on a question

to tell the story of The Procession of the Potato
that Gerardo Chávez painted on the humbleness of the sacks
with colored soils that he himself prepared, and that you almost
lost your right eye at the age of five
and to play Hopscotch
as if the road to heaven
were the road to poetry.
and there is only one day to rest
and to perceive in silence, while your family makes a pilgrimage
to Ancon,
to wash the clothes of your dead grandmother as
purification for her journey and she continues
living in each one of you, while
Gerardo Chavez

dibuja fieles monstruosos y el maya del cielo, que
nunca pensaron que resucitaría, ciertamente ha
resucitado, un reencarnado, un
redivivo del pueblo, una
hora cualquiera, antes
del maya del cielo que seguirá resucitando
con regularidad
para que siempre
la Comala de Pedro Páramo
siga creyéndose una fuerza miserable
donde la vida
que no se mide por años
ni es un espectáculo
impide que sepamos dónde está

abismarnos dentro de nosotros es inútil

hemos sido abandonados en un movimiento extraño
aquí la eternidad del árbol del hambre se desnuda,
protege al pájaro,
se despide de la guerra y la enfermedad
y la palabra que aún queda en mí
la despego de mi lengua
para regalársela al manantial

*Pero abro un agujero en mis células inmortales. Dibujo en su comienzo,
garabateo en su final. Retuerzo el papel en el que escribo sus nombres, las
convierto en aviones, en palomas.*

draws faithful monsters and the maya in the sky, which
they never thought would be resurrected, has certainly
been resurrected, one reincarnated, one
revived among the people, any
one given hour, before
the maya in the sky which will continue to resurrect
with regularity
so that always
the Comala of Pedro Páramo
will continue believing itself to be a miserable force
where life
which is not measured by years
nor is it a spectacle
prevents us from knowing where it's at

it is useless to plunge into ourselves as if into an abyss

we have been abandoned in a strange movement
here the eternity of the hunger tree is naked,
it protects the bird,
says goodbye to war and disease
and the word that still remains in me
I detach it from my tongue
to give as a gift to the water spring

But I open a hole in my immortal cells. I draw at its beginning, I scribble at its end. I twist the paper on which I write their names, turn them into airplanes, into pigeons.

SUTURA / SUTURE

Mi cáncer dice:

me hiciste como si yo fuera un poema. Tu lloro. Y entre lágrimas preguntabas: ¿quién podrá sanarme? Y yo vine a ti y no me viste y me fui y no me entendiste. Me volví entonces el silbo de alacranes azulados que con su canto intentaban repararte. Al final nos vimos a la cara y ya no reconocías a nadie. No sabías si eras digna de amor o de odio. Mas yo si te recordaba y por eso te abracé, te entregué un libro, te di escaleras, pero tú me empujaste y me pateaste y como una niña malcriada seguiste tu camino. Yo no quería verte muerta, pero quería quedarme contigo. Te había tomado afecto y me había acostumbrado a ti. Hoy te sigo viendo a lo lejos hablando al silencio, doblando tus sostenes, contando tus vestidos, sentada sobre tu cama, esperando a que se hagan las siete y llegue tu marido, tu única alegría en esta ciudad que te da tanto calor y tanto miedo. Me haces falta. Aunque ahora tienes luz y ya no más fe. Alguien desató las lenguas hermanas de nuestro beso. Alguien quiso que olvidaras mi nombre. Por eso hoy yo te pido: dilo, di mi nombre. Nómbrame por última vez.

Cánceres de tierra y de metal. Padezco y acepto el desconsuelo. El viento, infestado de polvo y piedras, golpea la casa del dormido y me llama al cielo del santo.

My cancer says:

you made me as if I were a poem. Your cries. And in tears, you asked: who will be able to heal me? And I came to you and you didn't see me and I left and you didn't understand me. I then became the whistling of azure scorpions that tried to fix you up with their song. In the end, we saw each other face to face and you no longer recognized anyone. You didn't know if you were worthy of love or hate. But I did remember you and that's why I hugged you, gave you a book, gave you stairs, but you pushed me and kicked me and like a spoiled little girl you went on your way. I didn't want to see you dead, but I wanted to stay with you. I had grown fond of you and I had gotten used to you. Today I still see you in the distance talking to the silence, folding your bras, counting your dresses, sitting on your bed, waiting for seven o'clock to come and for your husband to arrive, your only joy in this city that gives you so much heat and so much fear. I'm missing you. Though now you have light and no more faith. Someone untied the sister tongues of our kiss. Someone wanted you to forget my name. So today I ask of you: say it, say my name. Name me for the last time.

Cancers of earth and metal. I suffer and accept the grief. The wind, infested with dust and stones, blows the house of the sleeper and calls me into the heaven of saints.

CICATRIZ / SCAR

Estoy aquí frente a la nube sin saber qué preguntar.

Una fuerza extraña detrás de	la voluntad
Allí muere	la voluntad
Es como si	la voluntad
Mirara	al corazón
Pero detrás de	la voluntad
las personas se casan unas con otras desde niños	sin saberlo
quizá sea la familia el primer matrimonio	sin saberlo
el colegio el segundo	sin saberlo
la universidad el tercero	sin saberlo
y detrás	del corazón
un preso dialoga con su carcelero	sin saberlo

I stand here in front of the cloud unsure of what to ask.

A strange force behind	the will
There lies dead	the will
It is as if	the will
Looked through	the heart
But behind	the will
people marry each other since childhood	without knowing
perhaps the family is the first marriage	without knowing
school is the second	without knowing
college is the third	without knowing
and behind	the heart
a prisoner dialogues with his jailer	without knowing

una coreana reza junto a un senegalés   sin saberlo

como si   la voluntad

mirara siempre   con nostalgia   al corazón

Pero detrás   de la voluntad

las personas hacen el amor al mismo tiempo   sin saberlo

piden perdon todas juntas   sin saberlo

comen y orinan en comunión   sin saberlo

está pues   la bondad

contemplando hace siglos a   la felicidad

como San Agustín explicó al   amor

A Korean woman prays next to a Senegalese man   without knowing

as if   the will

would always looked   with nostalgia to   the heart

But behind   the will

people make love at the same time   without knowing

ask for forgiveness all together   without knowing

eat and piss in communion   without knowing

there is therefore   graciousness

for centuries contemplating   happiness

as saint Augustine explained   love

Pero detrás del   amor

las personas de distintas ciudades contraen la misma enfermedad

por su falta de   miedo

y detrás del   miedo

un tenor se queda afónico de tanto   pensamiento

y detrás del   pensamiento

una niña pierde en una plaza su   virtud

y detrás de   la virtud

explota la escuela de la   alegría

y detrás de   la alegría

un poeta rompe su poema sobre   la pasión

But behind   love

people in different cities contract the same disease

due to their lack of   fear

and behind   fear

a tenor becomes hoarse from so much   thinking

and behind   thinking

a little girl at a public square loses her   virtue

and behind   virtue

explodes the school of   joy

and behind   joy

a poet breaks his poem about   passion

y detrás de   la pasión

las mujeres hilan sombreros en   la amistad

como si no conocieran otra cosa más que eso en   la amistad

y detrás de   la amistad

una tetera de cerámica se rompe
con el agua caliente de   la belleza

y detrás de   la belleza

los obreros del mundo tienen parecidas las caras
como si el mal en su distancia
no formara parte   del mal

y detrás del   mal

un pequeño títere olvidado entre la basura

and behind   passion

women spin hats in   friendship

as if they knew nothing else but that in   friendship

and behind   friendship

a ceramic teapot breaks
with the hot water of   beauty

and behind   beauty

the workers of the world have similar faces
as if evils at a distance
were not part   of evil

and behind   evil

a little puppet forgotten among the garbage

Aquí estoy otra vez frente a la   voluntad

como muchas otras personas temerosas frente a la   voluntad

un diez de febrero a las siete de la tarde

El agua que sale de mi pecho vacío es tan poderosa como un manantial.

Here I am once again facing   the will

like many other fearful people facing   the will

on a tenth of February at seven o'clock in the evening

The water coming out of my empty chest is as powerful as a water spring.

AFTERWORD
by Silvia Goldman

Opening what? For what? To see what? Teresa Orbegoso's book invites us to entertain these questions, to listen to what language has to say to itself, so that it becomes the opposite of fear. A language present, one that opens and closes, one that breathes, and witnesses what still needs to be named. This book is about the existence of this language.

Teresa Orbegoso exists/ The cancer patient exists,

says the poetic voice, and adds:

> *Collapsed the tower of Babel exists*
> *September Eleventh exists*
> *the burnt ones of the war with Chile as discolored limbos*
> *also the six murdered and the forty-three missing students*
> *in Ayotzinapa*
> *as when*
> *the snoring of those who are buried underground*
> *wakes us up alarmed for the future of our children*
> *as if a war were*
> *painted with our legs, our arms, a shot*
> *[...]*

131

As if to say: the historical conditions that enable the emergence of cancer exist, trauma exists, the girl still *looking at it all* exists, the cancer that stems from a rhetoric of pain and exclusion also exists. And it is not an isolated event that afflicts an individual alone, it is a consequence of systemic and structural injustice. It is personal but also political. It is *The only Teresa among the old toys of the only girl in the only city surviving the last word.*

Cancer is a condition that requires that the gap between words and action be lessened. Hence, when the poetic voice tells us *my cancer says*, we witness its saying, we acknowledge its presence, we enter the room of the sick, we listen. We are inside an outside, a place where language has not yet entered, we become marginalized, excluded, we are outsiders, we are *it*. And precisely because of that we do what the book, in an overwhelming but urgent apostrophe, asks us to do: *listen to your cancer.*

Can a disease be also a gift, can it bring with it something precious, a message worth listening to, a language that enables a crack, an opening? What does it mean to open language to the experience of having cancer? Could it provide us with *a new purity, a revelation, the keys to suffering, something that looks for new words*, a possibility to speak differently, with the words we do not yet have, to speak not about it, but in it?

It is difficult to put the personal pronoun "I" near the word "cancer". The voice in this book does even more: she puts the possessive pronoun in front of a noun that is already uttered with difficulty. She says *my cancer*; she attaches the noun to the possessive, making the acquisition of the I unquestionable, undeniable. Thus, the *my* that rests on the *I* ties itself to the personal pronoun with a double knot. It clings to it, it establishes a logic of closeness and belonging that adheres like ointment to the writing. *My cancer says, I, my I, my*

132

cancer, the I of my cancer, the possibilities of language, like those of fear, open up, *stitch your story to mine,* they become the wound and the suture, a *cancerous* language that is not afraid of saying I.

There's a speed in words, as if there was an urgency to say, to accumulate all visible and invisible things, all possible and impossible meanings, take them all into the mouth, taste them *now,* in the very moment of the opening. There is a relationship between language and time. Language is fast –it has to be– in order to grow proportionally to that which needs to be looked at, touched, uttered. Not a clean, aseptic language, but a growing, *present* language that allows itself to observe, to become sick, and name its sickness. One that brings the past to the present, the collective to the individual, the political to the personal. A language that says *cancer* as many times as it needs to. It is a daring, bold, excessive language. It is as if cancer required this delivery, this accountability, this letting out, as a way of not dying.

Each time we open Orbegoso's book we listen to an opportunity in language, an opening, as in a prayer, precarious and precious, that asserts itself with every repetition. In the midst of the most terrible anxiety and anticipation, language becomes a presence, a present, a mode of *opening fear.* It says: I exist. She exists. You exist. It asserts its own existence and, also, that of the readers.

Wilmette, IL. August 2023

133

ABOUT THE AUTHOR

Teresa Orbegoso (Lima, 1976) Visual artist. Poet. Cultural journalist. Social researcher. Cultural organizer. Curator. She holds a degree in Journalism from the Universidad Jaime Bausate y Mesa (Peru) and a Master's Degree in Creative Writing from the Universidad Nacional de Tres de Febrero (Argentina). She has a diploma in Advertising Creativity and studies in Philosophy and Musical Creation: Traditional Arts and New Technologies. She has received scholarships from the OAS, INDES IDB and Tallberg Foundation to participate in seminars and workshops for social leaders organized in Brazil, Colombia, United States and Sweden (2001-2006). She has published the poetry collections *Yana wayra* (Lima, Urbano Marginal, 2011), *Mestiza* (Buenos Aires, Ediciones del Dock, 2012), *La mujer de la bestia* (Maldonado, Trópico Sur, 2014), *Yuyachkani* (together with visual artist Zenaida Cajahuaringa, Lima, La Purita Carne, 2015), *Perú* (Buenos Aires, Buenos Aires Poetry, 2016), *Comas* (Buenos Aires, Añosluz, 2018) and *Abro el miedo* (Lima, Hanan Harawi Editores, 2019; Argentina, Las Furias Editora, 2020). *Abro el Miedo / Opening Fear*, a testimonial poetry book about her experiences with cancer, was nominated for the Luces Prize from the Peruvian newspaper *El Comercio*, in the category "Best poetry book". In 2022 she received a grant from the Peruvian Ministry of Culture to present her books *Peru* and *Abro el miedo* at poetry festivals in Spain. Her poetry book *Perú* has been published in Mexico, Guatemala, Peru and Spain. Her work has been included in a number of academic studies in Chile, Mexico, the United States and Sweden. She has been invited to several poetry festivals in Latin America and her work has been included in various online magazines around the world. Her work has been included in anthologies of contemporary South American poetry in Argentina, Chile, Colombia and Peru. She has been director of the Casa Cultural - Espacio de Arte Trenzando Fuerzas, and currently runs the publishing house La Primera Vértebra and hosts the program "La danza de las libélulas" for the platform La mula in Lima, Peru together with the sociologist and therapist Marco Del Mastro. As a media producer, she has created a series of diverse materials that allow for the mediation between readers and the book, among which stand out: the music composed for the book *La casa sin sombra* by the Argentine writer Claudio Archubi; the videopoems made for her books *Yana wayra, La mujer de la bestia, Perú* and *Abro el miedo*; the podcast "Cuerpas" for the poetry journal La primera vértebra, and a cycle of interviews to Latin American writers for the Casa Cultural - Espacio de Arte Trenzando Fuerzas.

ABOUT THE CONTRIBUTORS

Vania Milla (Lima, 2005) is studying Communications at the University of Lima and intends to specialize in Journalism. She is an avid reader and enjoys spending her free time playing guitar and biking around the city. She began studying English at a young age and has a keen interest in translation as a means of bringing Spanish-language literary production to English-speaking readers. This is her first published translation.

Yaxkin Melchy Ramos (Mexico City, 1985) is a Mexican and Peruvian-Quechua poet, translator, ecopoetics researcher, and artisan-activist-editor. He is the author of *Poetechnics* (Cardboard House Press, 2023) and *The New World*, a five-part "constellation-book" which was written intermittently between 2007 and 2017. Currently he is a graduate student at Tsukuba University in Japan, where he is researching ecopoetic currents between Japan and Latin America. Since 2017, he has been translating contemporary Japanese poetry to Spanish, and currently he runs the artisanal press *Cactus del viento*, which focuses on ecological, spiritual, and transpacific poetics. He also publishes on his personal blog, *Flor de Amaneceres*. (Cardboard House Press).

Silvia Goldman (Montevideo, 1977), a native from Uruguay, received her PhD in Hispanic Studies from Brown University in 2011. She is currently working on the final stages of a book-length manuscript on contemporary Latin American Poetry entitled *La recuperación de la palabra en la poesía latinoamericana contemporánea*. She teaches all levels of Spanish language and culture. Her research and teaching interests include Hispanic poetry and poetics, creative writing, representations of madness in the Hispanic tradition, violence and repression in post-dictatorship Southern Cone, Transatlantic Studies, and the interplay between performance, memory, and cultural identity in Latin America. Silvia is also a poet. Her academic journals and poems have been published in journals such as *Revista Canadiense de Estudios Hispánicos, Rassegna Iberistica, RILCE, Inti, Maldoror: Revista de la ciudad de Montevideo, Nueva York Poetry Review, Plenamar, Conexos, TriQuarterly*, and *Revista de escritura y poéticas 7 de 7*. She is the author of three poetry collections: *Cinco movimientos del llanto* (Hermes criollo, 2008), *De los peces la sed* (Pandora Lobo Estepario 2018), and *miedo* (Axiara editions 2020). (DePaul University)

Margarita Saona studied linguistics and literature at Pontificia Universidad Católica del Peru. She received a Ph.D. in Latin American literature from Columbia University in New York. She is head of the department of Hispanic and Italian Studies at the University of Illinois. She is interested in issues of gender, memory, cognition, empathy, and representation in literature and the arts. She has published numerous articles, the books on literary and cultural criticism, *Novelas familiares: Figuraciones de la nación en la novela latinoamericana contemporánea* (Rosario, 2004) and *Memory Matters in Transitional Perú* (Londres, 2014), two books of short fiction, *Comehoras* (Lima, 2008) and *Objeto perdido* (Lima, 2012), and a book of poems, *Corazón de hojalata/Tin Heart* (Chicago, 2017). Her latest publications are *Despadre: Masculinidades, travestismos y ficciones de la ley en la literatura peruana* (Editorial Gafas Moradas, 2022), which deals on the representation of masculinity in Peruvian literature, and *La ciudad en que no estas* (Cocodrilo Ediciones, 2021) a collection of her short stories that has also been published in English as *The Ghost of You* (tr. Luciana Erregue, Laberinto Press, 2023.) (University of Illinois at Chicago)

Louise Castillo (Lima, Perú.) Photographer and graphic designer whose personal projects are an exploration of surrealism and human emotions. With a higher education in graphic design and a passion for photography, her work has developed a particular style that combines photography and digital experimentation. She began her career as a traditional photographer in 2017, but soon turned to editing and manipulation techniques that allow her to create new realities through images. Her creations cover a wide range of subjects that explore the boundaries of reality and the subconscious, and her works are known for their painterly aesthetic with a color palette inspired by baroque, renaissance and gothic art. She has collaborated in different artistic projects for renowned writers and independent musicians. She is currently working on the upcoming release of two projects, an e-book called "$-\infty$ e ∞" and her first solo exhibition.

www.ingramcontent.com/pod-product-compliance
Lightning Source LLC
Chambersburg PA
CBHW051652120626
46551CB00015B/2326